Look who's home
for dinner!

Look who's home for dinner!

A compact guide to owning and caring for a horse at your home or any other private property. From proper selection of fencing to feeding, and handling emergencies.

Marion Wright

iUniverse

LOOK WHO'S HOME FOR DINNER!

A compact guide to owning and caring for a horse at your home or any other private property. From proper selection of fencing to feeding, and handling emergencies.

iUniverse books may be ordered through booksellers or by contacting:

iUniverse
1663 Liberty Drive
Bloomington, IN 47403
www.iuniverse.com
1-800-Authors (1-800-288-4677)

ISBN: 978-1-4917-5329-3 (sc)
ISBN: 978-1-4917-5331-6 (e)

Printed in the United States of America.

iUniverse rev. date: 11/17/2014

This book is meant to support novice or first-time horse owners in finding the right answers to their questions and finding out what questions to ask to get the right answers!

Introduction

Horses are large animals and do require quite a bit of room. In the wild, horses move around constantly in pursuit of both pastures to graze on and water, which they need on a daily basis.

Domesticated horses are confined to a rather small area (in comparison), and we, as their humans, try to make them as comfortable as possible by providing them with large paddocks, turnouts, and regular exercise to keep them healthy and happy.

So, how much space does a horse really need? Is my garden fence good enough? After all, it seems to work for my neighbor's horse. Well, it all depends; not every horse is happy in the same environment, but there's a way to get pretty close.

This guide will certainly not answer all your questions, nor can it solve your specific problems. It is meant to give you an overview and basic guidelines to owning a horse and what you can expect in general when keeping a horse at home. Don't hesitate to call upon professional help if you are unsure about something. Trainers, veterinarians, and feed stores can often provide the information you need or point you in the right direction.

You will ultimately save yourself a lot of money and headaches by spending a comparatively small amount to get a qualified opinion and ask for help from a professional trainer or a veterinarian BEFORE you run into problems you can't handle by yourself.

Your horse will thank you by staying happier and healthier from the first day you welcome him into your life!

Chapter 1

How to prepare your property for a horse

Where should my horse live?

If your horse gets exercised or ridden <u>at least</u> 4 times a week, a 24'x24' corral will be sufficient for them to live in. However, in this case, bigger IS better. No horse will object to a large run or a grazing pasture as a living space. Shelters are important, not only to protect them from the rain in cold weather, but more importantly from the sun when it is blazing hot. Not all horses will use a shelter when it rains, but ALL horses will seek shade when it's hot.

How fancy you bed your horse beyond the basics is up to you. A run-in shed or box stall or a three-sided shelter with an attached run sounds like the Hilton to most horses. Rubber mats can aid in keeping the feeding area clean and free from sand and mud. When choosing the site for your horse's paddock or stall, you should also consider the watershed when it rains, and make sure your horse has a reasonably dry spot to lay down even in foul weather.

Do horses need buddies?

Horses are herd animals. As the potential prey they seek safety in numbers. Some horses are pretty cool about being an only horse and will be happy with other buddies such as goats, donkeys, or sometimes the human contact will be sufficient. But let's face it, your own species is always the best. So, if you are planning to have your horse at home, know that you will sooner or later add another one - or two - for their well-being.

FENCING

No matter what size corral or pasture you keep your horse in, it has to be "horse-proof". As a rule of thumb, if they can get hurt on it, they will. Horses have an uncanny ability to find protruding wire ends, nails on the ground, large slivers sticking out of a wooden pole or of getting their feet stuck in tight places. There are a few types of fencing that are recommended for horse structures, depending on the desired curb appeal and, of course, your budget.

Any fence will only be as good as the maintenance it receives. Be sure to check your fences frequently regardless of the material you are using. A horse that gets a hoof caught in a wire loop or between two boards will 9 out of 10 times struggle and break a leg or do severe damage to itself in the course of panicking to break free.

Steel panels

The most common way to contain horses is by use of pipe corrals, which are available at most feed stores or, for a better price, at specialized manufacturers. A lot of times these panels can be found for sale by private parties on websites such as www.craigslist.net or other classified sites geared towards horse owners.

Pipe corrals are usually sold in lengths of 12', 16' or 24' with a height of 5'. The number of horizontal rails can vary within the same height panel, creating a different spacing in between. 5 rails are the most popular variation, close enough together to prevent most horses from sticking their heads through (and thereby rubbing out their mane), but far enough apart not to lock in a leg that's accidentally stuck through the fence. They can be enhanced with a special wire grid which prevents neighboring horses from biting or kicking each other through the fence. However, 4 rails are usually sufficient and allow you to save some money on your purchase.

Wooden fencing

Admit it, wood just looks fancy. It's pretty, it's the classic ranch look, and your horse will love to chew on it! Horses have pretty strong teeth and they will get bored at times when you're not around. Since horses are designed to eat or graze for most of the day, they try to chew on odd things when there's no hay around. Wood is very inviting, they love the taste of it, and it is soft enough to actually give them a sense of accomplishment as far as the eating and chewing sensation goes. Not only will it be unsightly, but horses can end up with large slivers in their gums or anywhere on or in their bodies as a result. In addition the fence will lose its strength over time.

To use wood for fencing means to protect it from being chewed on either by an electrified reinforcement, added wire fencing, or special wood treatment/stain that makes it undesirable for horses.

Wire fencing

Wire has been used for years and years to contain all kinds of animals, so why would it be different with horses, right? Well, horses ARE different.

Unlike cows, horses can be of an explosive energy - fast moving and annoyingly silly at times. Barbwire or single strand wire injuries on horses range from de-gloved legs to severed muscle and ripped off ears. There are wire fences especially designed for horses, namely "No-climb" and "V-mesh" wire fencing. The mesh is designed to not let a hoof slip through and not let a horse get hold and step up onto the wire. However, as with all fences, regular checks are necessary to make sure there are no broken sections creating holes and loops that can catch a hoof or get stuck on the back of a horse's shoe when sticking a foot through.

Electric fencing

Electrically charged fences can be very effective to restrain horses to their respective living spaces. There are numerous designs and colors to choose from; many are able to be charged by small solar panels. Whichever design you choose, it should be a tape design rather than a single-strand wire, which used to be popular a few decades ago. Tape has better visibility for horses and it generally won't cause any injuries should they get entangled in it by accident. In addition, tape will break at a certain overload rather than strangle a horse or break a leg like a steel wire would. Remember that your horse will only respect your electric fence if it is "hot" at all times. If they learn that it may not be charged, they will start testing it and find out that it can be harmless and destroyed in minutes – which makes maintenance and daily checks key to success.

Plastic fencing

The new age vinyl plastic fences can give your property a very sleek look and can be effective as horse fencing - with some improvements. If you know your horse, you may be able to install these fences with no added modification; but it doesn't always prove to be enough for all eventualities. Vinyl tends to break on overload, leaving dangerous jagged edges, and the maximum strength of those rails will not withstand a testy horse trying to reach the grass on the other side or being the target of a vigorous butt-scratching session. However, your dainty little Arabian may be just fine and happy without challenging your installation. If you love the look, you can enhance the strength of those fences by mounting the standards in concrete and inserting wood into the top rails. The standards are designed to be slipped over a 4'x4' or a 2'x6' wooden board for increased strength, thus keeping the wood from getting wet and rotting over time.

DRAINAGE

Staying a step ahead of the rainy season in designing your horse property will save you a lot of hassle when the time comes. As long as your horses have a dry spot where they can eat and drink and stay out of the mud they will be fine. The sheltered area of your corral or paddock should be the highest point so the water or melting snow can drain away from their food area. Horses have to lay down to sleep every day, so ideally your dry area will accommodate enough room for them to take their daily beauty nap in a soft and dry spot.

Sure, having your horse live on the incline behind your house makes it easy on the drainage, but be prepared for your horse slipping and falling when the footing gets wet and slippery as they satisfy their urge to move around, even in bad weather. Every paddock should have a flat portion for the horses where they can get out of the weather and move their feet without sliding off a cliff.

To prevent mud or improve the footing in the horse area you can add screened sand and/or DG (decomposed granite) in order to provide a mud-free environment. Note that old horse manure will turn into "quick-mud" when wet, so keep your stalls clean to prevent both an awful mess and hoof problems going along with the wet seasons. Another option for rain absorbing footing is CedaRestTM, which can be quite an initial investment for a larger area but which will make the rainy season a breeze! You can easily find lots of information online or by asking your local feed store.

MANURE MANAGEMENT

Horses eat a lot and poop a lot. Their waste is easy to compost and makes great fertilizer once it is broken down. However, the amount of horse manure will probably exceed your own needs at some point and you will have to think about ways to get rid of it. Manure from one or two horses can be taken care of by your local waste management company by means of a 2-yard container emptied once a week. If you have a local farm e.g., worm farms or nursery around they might be interested in some or all of your manure as fertilizer as long as it's clean and free from any trash; it's always worth asking. Even though I don't generally recommend this, you can use dry manure to soften the footing in your arena if you are on a tight budget. In order to be effective it has to be mixed in with the existing footing (dirt or sand) by means of a rototiller or a good harrow, and it will make the arena nice and soft to ride in. The disadvantage is that as soon as it rains it will turn into "quick-mud" and be very slippery. To keep a good balance do not allow more manure than sand in the mix and keep your local climate in mind. It may mean that your arena may be nice to ride in when you control your horse's movements but won't be a good choice for a turnout paddock anymore in wet weather when they run free and go slipping and sliding.

To answer the million-dollar question: Yes! You should definitely remove the manure from your horses' pen/corral! Manure attracts flies and will also prevent the paddock from drying out properly. After a decent rainfall you will otherwise discover that your horse is standing knee deep in poop, which will promote fungus, hoof rot, and the growth of all kinds of bacteria. At the very least remove it from the corral and spread it on the property as fertilizer, or pile it up and advertise it for free. Your horse will be healthier for it and – let's face it – who deserves to live in an outhouse?

PLANTS

Horses are usually picky eaters when it comes to grazing, but they are also curious creatures; and most of them will nibble on fallen leaves or little twigs that get blown into their paddock once their daily hay is devoured. Toxic plants don't usually taste good and most horses will avoid them, but you can't leave the decision solely up to their instincts when they're hungry or bored. Some of these plants are poisonous to horses in small amounts and can cause anything from a slight tummy ache to death.

Different climates produce different plants and trees and it is best to familiarize yourself with the most common toxic plants in your particular area. Your local veterinarian can advise you on toxic plants and trees in your climate, and there is ample information available on the internet. Please remember to rely only on reputable sources when researching facts online, e.g., a university library site versus a gardening website blog. I will list the most common toxic plants (source: University of California, Davis); but as a rule of thumb for the botanically challenged you would be advised to be suspicious of any bush, shrub, or tree that produces pretty flowers or has a pungent odor (e.g., rhododendrons, azaleas, oleander) Stay away from anything that a hotel would plant to add curb appeal.

Most common poisonous plants in order of toxicity level:

- Yew (taxus species)
- Oleander (nerium oleander)
- Red maple (acer rubrum)
- Cherry trees and relatives (prunus species)
- Black walnut (juglans nigra)
- Black locust (robinia pseudoacacia)
- Horse chestnut, Buckeyes (aesculus hippocastanum)
- Oak trees, acorns (quercus species)
- Russian olive / Oleaster (elaegnus angustifolia)

There are some very useful online resources to identify poisonous plants, provided by universities and private organizations. Below are a few links to online catalogs that can help you recognize toxic plants and also describe their effects on horses *http://cal.vet.upenn. edu/projects/poison/index.html* *http://www.understanding-horse-nutrition.com/poisonous-plants.html* *http://njaes.rutgers.edu/pubs/ fs938/* (includes photos for identification) *http://www.raspberryridge. com/Feature-Poisonous%20plants.htm* (very comprehensive with photos and symptoms)

Not all plants need to be ingested to cause a toxic reaction in horses. For example black walnut is extremely toxic to horses if it is present in wood shavings used as bedding. The oil contained in this tree species can cause severe and sudden laminitis in your horse after just a few hours of exposure. This tree is not all too common in California but is used in the furniture industry and occasionally as an accent tree in landscaping. If you're not sure where your shavings come from always ask if it contains black walnut.

If you are not sure about the toxicity of a plant, check with an equine veterinarian or do the safe thing and get rid of it. Just because your horses are not usually near a poisonous plant or tree doesn't mean they won't have access. Fallen leaves can blow into their paddock, or maybe your horse will one day escape into your yard and just give the new variety a try.

<u>SUMMARY</u>

These basic guidelines should help you to create a safe environment for your equine friend. Remember that all horses are different and have different characters and personalities, just like people do. A fiery thoroughbred will need more room and exercise than a lazy and quiet quarter horse. Many times a conversation with the seller of your newly purchased horse can help you create the right living quarters for your new horse, and a veterinarian is always a good source for information on how to keep a horse healthy.

Chapter 2

How to care for your horse

INTRODUCTION

Horses have a long history of being domesticated and have always been of great value to mankind, primarily as means of transportation or as pure horse power. Often a horse was a man's most valuable possession and, as such, well cared for.

Buying a horse is often the smallest expense. A lot of people forget to consider how much the upkeep of a horse can cost, especially when dealing with rescues or neglected horses and, of course, your run-of-the-mill emergency. We will discuss here what caring for a horse means, what cost to expect and, if money is an issue, where to save it to the horse's best advantage.

What are my expenses?

A horse will need three things to be healthy and happy that cannot be missed.

1. Food
2. Farrier service and

3. Vaccines / other veterinary care

FOOD

In the wild, horses graze on average about 18 to 22 hours per day. In a perfect (domesticated) world a horse should have access to free choice grass hay (NOT alfalfa). However, if your horse's exercise is limited you may be owning the equivalent of a whale in a short amount of time. Diet and nutrition are as individual for horses as they are for humans. Following are some examples and recommendations.

Fresh Grass / Pasture

Obviously horses are designed to live on grazing pastures, but not all of us are fortunate enough to provide paradise for our equine pals. In some parts of the country grazing is a luxury; some horses don't even know what fresh grass is. If you do have an irrigated grass pasture, don't expect your horse to be fat and happy eating just that. Horses are picky eaters; they will not eat weeds and they usually don't "mow" the grass either. They prefer the fresh young blades and leave the old thick grass until there's no other choice. In order to have a healthy horse on a grass pasture diet, you need to make sure there is the right grass mix seeded out, no toxic plants or undesirable weeds (although some weeds provide a variety in grazing), and there needs to be enough space per horse to avoid over-grazing. (usually minimum of 1 acre per horse). It can be done, but it involves serious planning and soil samples to make sure horses don't overdose on any minerals present in the plants. So unless you really have the space and the know-how, grass pastures should be considered a past-time and a place of relaxation and snack time for your horse. It will make any horse happy to get some grazing time, be it in a corral or on the lead line. It is good for their stomachs, good for their minds, and keeps them from getting bored, which often equals mischief.

Fresh grass, especially in the spring, needs to be introduced gradually (1hr/day for a week, then extend to two hours, etc.), even more so if your horse is not used to fresh grass. Serious health problems, such as laminitis and founder, can occur as a result of overeating luscious spring or fall grass. Please consult a veterinarian for detailed information and risks if you are not familiar with the effect grass can have on horses that are not used to it.

Please do NOT feed your horse lawn mower clippings. The heat from the blade and the fact that the grass gets centrifuged at high speeds makes it very unattractive to horses and it ferments extremely quickly, which can cause colic. On the other hand, weed trimmed grass can be acceptable, always being aware of the actual plants you are cutting and then feeding to your horses.

HOW MUCH SHOULD I FEED MY HORSE?

You can feed your horse very accurately by pound if he needs to be on a strict diet, or you can let your horse have access to hay all day. You should get information about your horse's usual diet from the seller and then use good judgment to either continue with that same regimen or make changes for the benefit of the horse. If you have reason to doubt the seller's advice on how to feed your new horse, you should ask a veterinarian or a trainer to help you with your horse's dietary needs.

Ideally your horse should not be overweight or underweight, but sometimes that can be difficult to balance. Generally, a horse that is under 3 years old can be a bit lean to prevent joint problems due to excessive growth spurts or overweight.

The degree of visibility of the ribs is only one of the indicators of a horse's weight. If a horse is well fed you should not see the ribs under his coat unless he is moving and bending his body. Any horse that has clearly visible ribs and hip bones is underweight and needs more food.

If a horse is overweight you will not only not see the ribs, you also won't feel them if you place your hand on its rib cage. Fat pockets will deposit usually above the tail, over the ribs, on the crest of the neck and in front of the shoulders. If a horse is all 'curves' and can't turn his head without creating walrus-like rolls along the side of the neck it is probably time to change up the food intake. Obesity in horses can lead to laminitis and ultimately result in having to put them to sleep.

Sometimes a horse with a very shaggy winter coat can look fat, but in fact there is more hair than meat on its ribs. Make sure to always touch your horse's rib cage and rump when trying to check on his weight in the winter time. When the temperatures drop, the winter coat puffs up another size or two making your horse look super fluffy when in reality he needs to eat more. The digestion of food creates heat in the body, making it necessary to sometimes double the food in very cold temperatures just to keep the horse warm.

Exercise of course plays a large role in the amount of food your horse needs. Once you have a good feel for the ideal weight of your horse, you can increase or decrease his grain or hay as soon as you notice a change in his appearance or when you make changes in his exercise regimen. Make sure to allow two to three weeks before expecting to see any results of his new diet.

<u>HAY</u>

The type of hay available in your area depends on the climate and the soil, but as a rule you should choose a grass type of hay as the main staple of your horse's diet. Your veterinarian can advise you on what your horse should eat, especially if you rescued a horse that needs to gain weight, which has to be done slowly and carefully to prevent digestive problems.

<u>Bermuda Hay</u>

Bermuda hay can usually be fed without any hesitation to any horse unless there is an underlying medical issue, e.g., allergies, respiratory problem. It is the most available and most cost effective grass hay in the southwestern United States, but it may not provide all the nutrition for every horse and may have to be supplemented. Bermuda hay varies quite often in quality throughout the seasons and the amount of food may have to be adjusted according to the quality of the cutting. It should be the basis of your feeding rations. This hay can be offered free choice without risk.

Some breeds (drafts, ponies, some Spanish breeds) are prone to a condition called "insulin resistance," in which case the starch and sugar contents in their diet play a big role, not the protein. This is the only time bermuda hay is the worst possible hay to feed because of the high starch content, which is also present in all grain hay such as wheat, barley, rye or oat hay. Consult a veterinarian if you're not familiar with the symptoms of insulin resistance.

Alfalfa Hay

Alfalfa is not a grass hay, but a legume. As a matter of fact, it is actually cow food rather than horse food. However, horses absolutely love the sweet alfalfa hay and we - horse owners - have been using it for years to add weight and energy to our horses. Due to the high protein content, not every horse will react the same to being fed alfalfa. While one horse may just gain weight eating it and not change otherwise, another horse may start to get "hot," meaning that the energy level is raised; the horse may become nervous, spooky, irritable or even develop stall habits, such as pacing. Also, due to the high calcium content in alfalfa, it should not be fed in excess to foals or young horses that are not fully grown.

A balanced bermuda/alfalfa diet is not a bad choice, but know that you can regulate your horse's behavior and energy level with the amount of alfalfa that you are feeding. Because alfalfa is used for dairy cattle it is produced in abundance, comes in many quality choices, and can sometimes be cheaper than bermuda. It should not be a reason to feed your horse a straight alfalfa diet, which can have serious health risks.

Alfalfa should never be offered as a free choice hay. Health risks due to overfeeding can include stocked up (swollen) legs, muscle spasms, diarrhea, tying up (a serious muscle condition), gastrointestinal stones, laminitis, and - worst case scenario – founder, which can result in death. Ponies are inherently sensitive to alfalfa and founder easily, but most horses can be fed alfalfa with care. If you do not know the diet of a new horse try your local choice of grass hay first and add alfalfa slowly in increasing amounts, watching for changes in their behavior and well-being. In addition, alfalfa grown and processed in southern and midwestern states is prone to being invaded by blister beetles, which are highly poisonous. If your horse ingests a number of blister beetles that were processed with the alfalfa it will result in severe reactions and often death within a few hours. Make sure you know where your hay comes from and ask the right questions before buying!

Timothy Hay / Orchard Hay

Timothy and orchard hay are both low in protein, but very tasty and nutritious hay varieties, which can be fed as a sole source of hay (roughage) instead of bermuda hay, and can also be offered as free choice hay. These hay varieties are difficult to grow in California and therefore rather pricey, which usually puts a lid on free feeding it, but more popular and accessible in wetter climates such as the midwest. You will definitely do your horse a favor choosing timothy or orchard hay or similar hay varieties over bermuda, but consider the possibility of additional cost of feed and a horse that will turn up its nose when being served a less tasty hay.

Oat Hay

Usually rather affordable and widely available, oat hay can be a great addition to your horse's diet. Oat hay is the grassy stem including the actual oats, but harvested when still somewhat green. Nonetheless, the oats come with the hay. Your horse will love it, but may become very energetic if fed oat hay as part of a regular diet. If that is a desired effect, there is no reason not to feed it, as it has a lot of nutrition besides the oats. Since the oats and the leaves are the tastiest part, not all horses will clean up the stems and you might end up with a lot of waste. It is certainly a great snack and a good past-time because it keeps the horses busy with hunting down the little grain kernels in the pile of hay.

Barley Hay / Rye Hay

Similar to oat hay, but may not be as available.

3-way / 4-way Hay

Usually a mix of alfalfa, oat, rye, and orchard or timothy, but can vary locally. Can be a good balanced diet for horses that are in training or work every day and need the energy.

PELLETED FEED AND GRAIN

Nowadays the term "grain" is used rather loosely and describes any supplemental pelleted horse food, regardless if it contains actual grain kernels or not. Most horses can be healthy and well fed on a balanced hay diet and don't need grain or supplements in addition. However, if you are preparing your horse for show, do a strenuous workout every day, or have an older horse, grain can become a necessity to maintain weight and fitness level. Some horses are just not easy keepers and require more calories than the hay can provide in order to put meat on their ribs. The choice of grain is usually driven by the need to either add weight or energy. I will list the most common types of grain, but consider that there are numerous manufacturers that produce similar types of feed.

Senior Feed - Weight

Most feed companies offer a 'junior', 'adult', and 'senior' variety of equine feed. I have found that the 'Senior' variety of grain helps maintain the weight, but doesn't add too much energy. It's a good choice for supplementing the hard keeper or in fact, an older horse.

Adult Feed - Energy

This variety is usually the choice for a working horse with a regular workout, building muscle and needing more energy. Show horses, performance horses, and horses that could use a little more "go" are good candidates for this type of food.

Hay Pellets – Weight/Energy

Hay pellets come in many varieties. They are a good way to supplement a hay diet with a different type of hay without the mess and little to no wasting of hay. Alfalfa/bermuda blend pellets, orchard pellets, or other varieties are available at most feed stores. For older horses that have trouble with chewing or are prone to choking, these pellets can be soaked in water to make a mash and be fed instead of hay altogether.

Rice Bran - Weight

This is a great and usually rather inexpensive way to add weight and enhance the coat on any horse. Rice bran is the fatty part of the rice kernel, usually in powder form, but also available as a stabilized pelleted product. At a fat content of around 20%, it adds calories to a diet and gives a shiny coat. It's very sweet and horses love it, which makes it a great food to mix medication into.

Wheat Bran - Digestion

A sweet tasting flaky supplement, much like oatmeal or cream of wheat, wheat bran can be given as a treat or to hide medication in. Horses usually love it and will remind you of little kids when digging into the bowl and making a mess of themselves. Just like with oatmeal, water should be added to wheat bran before feeding it. It stimulates the intestines, but not all horses react well to it; some actually might get a stomach ache. So if your horse starts refusing the tasty treat it may have made the connection between the food and not feeling well after eating it.

Beet Pulp – Weight/Digestion

Beet pulp is becoming more popular and is also an inexpensive food addition for hard keepers. I personally love to feed beet pulp to all my horses because it can help to prevent sand colics. Beet pulp is a by-product of the sugar industry after the sugar beets have been processed and the sugar has been extracted. Still slightly sweet in taste, horses tend to love it. Since it is all fiber, it can also transport sand out of the horses' intestines and thereby help prevent sand colics, which can be an issue wherever horses eat off the ground and ingest sand or dirt along with their hay on a daily basis. It is also a very cost effective way to put weight but not excessive energy on a horse. It is available in a shredded or a pelleted form. Both **MUST** be soaked in water for a considerable amount of time. Dried shredded beet pulp must be soaked for at least 10 minutes; pelleted beet pulp for about 4-6 hours. Soak shredded beet pulp with twice the amount of water, and pelleted beet pulp with 3-4 times the amount of water. The exact amount will vary with your local feed supplier's products. You can speed up the soaking time by using hot water rather than cold. As long as there are no hard pellets left in the bucket it can be fed safely. **Never feed beet pulp dry, it can cause severe impaction and - worst case scenario - death by swelling up and blocking the horses' intestines.**

Whole Grains

Feeding a horse the proverbial oats will also make them "feel the oats"! Be selective in feeding any grain and only feed it if you know your horse will have a chance to work off the added energy. Introduce grains slowly – as with all feed changes - and watch for changes in your horse's behavior. Some can't handle straight grains; they may become restless, pacing, obnoxious, hard to handle, and display some other unwanted behavior under saddle. If you do choose to feed your horse grains you should choose the crushed (or crimped) version to increase palatability and nutritional value.

Supplements

Most horses don't have a need to receive extra supplements (vitamins, joint formulas, etc.) besides what is already provided with their regular hay diet. If your horse receives a processed horse food ration, there will be added vitamins contained in the feed as well. Horse supplements are as manifold as human supplements. The three biggest categories are hoof supplements (to promote a healthy or increased hoof growth), joint supplements (to improve mobility and/or ease arthritic conditions), and performance supplements (increased energy, improved oxygen use, etc.). Supplements can be expensive and without a monitored regulation system you are pretty much at the manufacturer's mercy as far as the promised efficacy goes. If you are looking for a supplement to help your horse with a health condition or any other problems you would do best to consult a veterinarian to recommend a supplement to you. Some supplements are more potent (less diluted) than others and therefore more effective. You may also choose to ask a local trainer for advice as trainers usually have experience with a very wide variety of them.

Treats

We all want to spoil our horses by feeding them tasty stuff. It's a great way to reward them for a job well done and can be used as an incentive for good behavior or simply to come to the gate instead of chasing after them. Besides the obvious treats, such as carrots, any store-bought horse cookies or even your own crafty creations created from online recipes, you can offer your horse any type of fruit. Not every horse is curious enough to give them a try, but popular snacks are not only apples or maybe pears, but also bananas (with or without peel), oranges (can be fed whole), peaches and – usually a favorite – watermelons or watermelon rinds – which should be cut into small pieces to prevent choke.

Please consider that these items are not on your horse's natural diet and should be fed in small amounts. Feeding a horse two pounds or more of any type of cookie or fruit can seriously upset his stomach or make them sick, so make sure to let common sense be your guide and don't overwhelm your horse with tasty treats at his own choosing.

Feeding Intervals and Tips

Ideally your horses will be most comfortable with being fed 3 times/ day - breakfast, lunch, and dinner - the dinner portion being the largest amount, since your horse has to bridge more time until the next meal. However, if you are not able to feed your horse lunch, two meals per day will be sufficient, trying to keep them 12 hours apart as best you can. Again, the dinner portion should be the larger amount if your horse has to wait longer for his breakfast and especially if the nights are getting colder.

When temperatures drop in the winter, you can help your horse stay warmer during the night by feeding his alfalfa portion in the evening or increasing the food if you notice your horse is losing weight. Alfalfa creates more body heat when being digested and can aid your horse in staying comfortable in freezing temperatures.

Food Placement

If you live in a very changing climate, you may want to provide food and water for your horses under their shelter or inside their stalls. Most horses will be comfortable eating their hay from the ground, although this can result in a lot of wasted hay and a muddy tar pit after the rainy season. It is cleaner to feed your horses from a feeding tub, hay net, or an above-ground feeder. The latest trend of slow feeders aids in creating a simulated grazing condition for your horse. This means that your horse will spend many hours picking at and eating the same amount of hay that would be devoured much faster if available in a trough. It will keep them busy and it can help prevent boredom and gastric ulcers or other digestive problems. Rubber mats covering the ground where they eat can help prevent the hay from being wasted and keep your horses from ingesting sand and dirt along with their food, which can over time accumulate in their intestines and cause a so-called sand colic.

Water

Horses need about 10-12 gallons of water per day and 20-25 gallons in hot weather. They are much pickier about clean water than dogs or cows. They can also be very susceptible to minerals contained in the water, sometimes being the cause of intestinal stones.

Automatic Waterers:

They come in several different types and are available at feed stores where the staff can recommend the right choice for your personal situation.

Advantages:

Automatic waterers can be a great time saver because they don't need to be refilled, water doesn't get stagnant and keeps flowing. They also won't grow algae at the same rate as a bucket or a larger water trough. They still need to be emptied and cleaned periodically. You can purchase heated waterers that won't freeze over in the winter, eliminating one disadvantage of these waterers in colder climates.

Disadvantages:

They do need to be monitored as some horses use them as scratching posts and might break the connectors. Sometimes you may even find manure in there, which of course means your horse won't be drinking until the water is clean again. Some horses like to dip their hay into the water when eating, which can clog the waterer and turn the water into green slime, which of course your horse will refuse to drink.

You will also have to make sure that the water in the pipes won't freeze in cold temperatures, cutting your horse's water supply off. On the other hand, if the pipes are all above ground and the waterer is in full sunlight, the water can actually get piping hot in the summer and your horse won't drink to avoid burning its sensitive muzzle.

When your horse is sick and you would really like to know how much he drinks or if he drinks at all, you should turn the waterer off and temporarily use a large bucket to monitor his water intake.

Buckets or Troughs

Advantages:

Buckets or larger troughs can be very practical because you can choose a size large enough for your horse(s) to share in a common pasture and you can also combine them with a float valve, so they keep refilling themselves to the desired water level. You don't have to worry about your horses running out of water just because you have a break in the waterline and the water won't be turned on again until tomorrow. Because of the large amount of water you don't need to worry about the water getting too hot in the summer. This only applies if you choose a larger size tank for your horses. More commonly for a single horse in a stall you can use a 10 gallon bucket or two in the summer if you can't refill them during the day.

Disadvantages:

If your horse happens to tip the bucket over while you're away, he won't have water all day and can become rather dehydrated. Algae will be a problem in the summer; a shady spot will slow down algae growth and keep the water cleaner longer. Anything smaller than 25-35 gallons should be emptied and refilled every day. On larger tanks you need to remove floating hay, bugs and other foreign matter by scooping off the surface with a bucket or maybe a fish net; and once a week (depending on your area and the size of the trough) the tank will need to be emptied, scrubbed, and refilled with fresh water, preferably without flooding your horse's corral in the process.

Occasionally squirrels or other animals will meet their demise in your horse's trough because they fell in and couldn't reach the edge to climb out. Always replace the water after such an incident because of the bacteria and possible parasites deposited in the water. A higher water level or a piece of rope tied to the tank wall can help prevent them from drowning or you can place a water bowl on the ground away from your horse for those critters.

If the conditions are supportive, you might be able to keep fish in your large pasture tank to control the algae and mosquito larvae. A pet store can advise you on the tank size and the type of fish you need for your area and climate. Horses will get used to the fish swimming around under their noses and quickly learn to ignore them.

In cold temperatures you will have to de-ice the water and find a way to keep the surface ice-free. There are many tanks on the market that offer a battery or even a power driven heater so the water is prevented from freezing. I highly recommend reading online reviews of technically demanding items to make sure that they don't turn out to be more hassle than benefit.

Any time your horse has been without water for a full day or longer, DO NOT let them drink too much at once or your horse might colic. Let them take 3-4 swallows and then wait a few minutes to let them make another few sips. The longer they have been without water, the slower they have to re-hydrate their body. If you have an automatic waterer, you can reduce the flow to slow down the refill rate to make your horse drink slower during the first hour. Remember that horses cannot vomit to relieve themselves of a tummy ache! It will always result in what we sum up as colic and will potentially require veterinary assistance.

FARRIER SERVICE

Every horse needs his hooves trimmed or shod regularly. How often depends on a variety of factors such as amount of exercise, food, and the terrain your horse is moving in, but usually the time period between farrier visits should be anywhere from 5-8 weeks.

Trim or shoe?

It is definitely cheaper to have a horse go barefoot than having to shoe it. and most horses should be just fine without shoes. However, not every horse is a candidate for going barefoot. Barefoot horses can be more sensitive to the ground than shod horses, just like the difference for people in going barefoot or wearing shoes. Your farrier should tell you if your horse can go barefoot or not. Even if your horse had shoes on all four hooves when you bought him, there is no reason not to try having him go barefoot unless the seller gave you a good reason to keep him shod.

Remember that a horse, just like a person, has to get used to going barefoot if it has worn shoes for a period of time. It can sometimes take up to 6 months until the hooves get hard enough to make your horse comfortable without shoes. If he is sensitive to rocks or hard ground during this time, you can purchase some protective hoof boots online that are designed to protect the hooves while riding and thus prevent the horse from feeling sore or from bruising on hard ground or rocky terrain. There are a variety of manufacturers that produce different styles of these hoof boots. Depending on how your horse's hoof is built, one or the other brand might provide a better fit.

Shoes will make sense with many horses that cannot go barefoot for a multitude of reasons. Some horses pace in their stalls and wear their feet very unevenly in the process, some paw at every occasion and wear their toes down, and some horses need shoes because their conformation (straightness of the legs) is not perfect and their hooves would wear in a way that would compromise the joints. Of course, if your horse has a career as a show horse, shoes can improve the performance and make your horse's job easier. If you are undecided, it is probably a good idea to ask a local trainer or a farrier for advice.

If your horse shares its living space with other horses, it is a good idea not to have their hind feet shod as any kick that is delivered to another horse will potentially result in serious injury or possibly broken bones rather than just a nasty bruise. Even a gentle horse can kick out due to being surprised or startled, and accidents happen faster than you can dial your veterinarian's number!

Make sure that your horse gets his hooves trimmed or shod in the recommended intervals. Long toes and grown out hooves can make your horse lame because of the strain on the joints and also cause irreversible damage to tendons and ligaments. No foot, no horse! Your horse will thank you for your diligence.

<u>GROOMING</u>

Don't forget to groom your horse! If your horse is out on a pasture or a large paddock, make it a habit to look him over at feeding time to make sure there are no wounds, injuries, swollen legs or sudden lameness issues. Grooming is certainly something that horses in the wild have to take care of themselves by means of scratching on trees or bushes or grooming each other with their teeth, rolling in the dirt or mud, and other innovative methods to rid themselves of dead hair and parasites.

Our domesticated horses need help with these tasks since often there are no buddies or trees available when they are kept in stalls or paddocks. Brushing off the loose hair, and picking out their hooves (or at least checking them for rocks or other foreign debris) is something that will help your horse stay happy and healthy. It is a good way to bond with your horse and establish a relationship, and almost all horses enjoy the grooming and brushing. In the winter horses need to be able to "fluff up" their hair coat to stay warm. If their fur is caked with mud, that won't be possible, and they will have a harder time regulating their temperature.

Bathing with shampoo should not be a daily event as it dries out the skin and removes necessary oils which can cause itchy, flaky skin and encourages your horse to scratch on any available surface. When bathing your horse, use a shampoo manufactured especially for horses (or baby shampoo) and be careful not to spray water into their ears. Showers with plain water on the other hand are often a welcome treat on hot days; some horses even love to stand in the sprinkler path to cool off or bathe in a pond if they have access.

VACCINATIONS

Every horse should be vaccinated to prevent the most common diseases and infections. Regardless of how you use your horse, if he's in your backyard, in a boarding stable, or on a pasture, vaccinations are absolutely essential to a horse's health. If you are comfortable giving vaccinations yourself (your local veterinarian can show you how), you can save some money by buying them at your local feed store or ordering them online and administering them at home. There are some vaccinations that are commonly administered once a year; some vaccines require a booster after 6 months. A lot of times your horse has already formed antibodies from earlier vaccinations and your veterinarian can run a test to find out if a vaccine would even be necessary.

West Nile: to protect from West Nile virus (requires a ground immunization)

3-way / 4-way / or 5-way vaccine: (tetanus, eastern and western encephalitis, rhinopneumonitis, and equine influenza) – Your veterinarian can advise you what your horse needs pertaining to your specific location, especially if your equine friend is a senior.

Besides these two vaccines and some variations thereof, there are also other immunizations available that are optional or only necessary if there is an epidemic on the loose or if your horse is about to travel or attend a show. Please consult a veterinarian to inform yourself about the details of vaccinating your horse as age, location and overall condition of your horse will play a role in which vaccines should or shouldn't be given. As an alternative, your veterinarian can advise you on ways to boost your horse's immune system as a preventive measure.

DEWORMING

De-worming is absolutely necessary in the summer, but also imperative in the winter since the parasites don't die off in milder weather. The more contact your horse has with other equines, the more important it is to deworm him regularly. 3-month intervals are recommended with varying dewormer ingredients to prevent the worms from building up resistance to one specific medication. Horses that suffer from worm infestation usually display a dull, rough coat, "leftover" winter coat that won't shed, low bodyweight and, especially noticeable in younger horses, a so-called "worm-belly," which looks very round and bloated. In some cases horses can become very sluggish and reluctant to move.

If you pay attention to the fresh manure and you spot worms, your horse definitely has a serious problem. In severe cases (e.g., if you rescued your horse from a case of neglect) you should consult a veterinarian for a professional opinion about deworming since horses can sometimes colic simply because of the sheer amount of dead worms being released from their intestines all at once. You can also ask your veterinarian to examine some fresh manure under the microscope for a fecal parasite count to make sure you don't administer chemical deworming agents that your horse does not need. As an alternative to chemical dewormers, there are also natural solutions, such as diatomaceous earth, which is available in feed stores or health food stores. You can easily look up its use online.

Chapter 3

How to deal with Emergencies

INTRODUCTION

Horses, despite their size, can be quite fragile animals. Their flight instinct can easily send them into panic mode making them forget their surroundings, and they are prone to injuries. Their digestive tracts are highly sensitive and we as horse owners need to take responsibility in considering their diet and care for removing them from their natural way of life.

In order to provide proper first aid, it is useful to know what would be considered an emergency and when to call a veterinarian rather than taking matters into your own hands. Your personal level of experience will greatly matter in aiding in your decision, but it is certainly never a bad idea to call a veterinarian and err on the safe side. Most veterinarians will try to assess the situation over the phone and let you know if it is necessary for them to come to see your horse, especially if you already have a relationship with them. The accuracy of your description will be key in the correct advice and assessing the severity of the situation over the phone. This will only be a brief overview of the most common injuries and sicknesses that you may encounter.

Leg injuries - Wounds

The most common injuries happen to a horse's legs. Just like people, some horses are clumsier than others and tend to get hurt more often regardless of how hard you try to provide a safe environment. If you are doing everything right, don't take it personal, but any horse can get his legs stuck under the pipe corral while rolling in the dirt. If you own a horse, you inevitably will have to deal with injuries down the line.

It is a very good idea to find a trainer or a veterinarian who is willing to give you a lesson on how to treat injuries -- most importantly, how to correctly wrap a horse's leg. Horses spend most of their lives on their legs -- they paw, dig, kick and play using their legs -- and most injuries will be in the form of cuts, lacerations, swellings or, more seriously, tendon or ligament injuries, or even fractures to their legs. With their tendons being rather exposed without any flesh to cushion them, cuts to the legs can potentially have quite detrimental consequences.

Any bleeding wound of course, regardless of its location, needs to be assessed, disinfected and dressed with ointment or (especially in the summer) with fly-repelling ointment to prevent fly infestation of the wound.

The large amount of blood resulting from a leg wound can be quite deceiving; always clean a wound out with clean water (with a hose or a clean sponge) to see how large of an injury you're actually dealing with before panicking. A lot of times it can help to clip the hair around the wound to better assess the severity and also to keep it cleaner during treatment.

If you are wondering if it needs to be stitched, it's probably a good idea to call the veterinarian. Remember that a wound can only be stitched within the first 4-6 hours after the injury occurred. After that the skin edges start to lose blood supply and stitching might no longer be an option. So if you're in doubt, know that changing your mind later is not a good idea; call the vet while you're still ahead of the game.

Because of the lack of fleshy tissue, any leg wound is prone to so-called "proud flesh", which is easily recognized. Proud flesh is excessive granulation tissue, bright pink in color, with a cauliflower-like appearance, which prevents the wound from healing. The healthy tissue cannot reconnect because it keeps the skin edges from rebuilding and closing over the injury. Proud flesh can be prevented in most cases by wrapping any leg wound with a bandage until the skin has closed over the wound.

Wrapping a horse's leg can be tricky: too loose of a bandage and it won't stay on, too tight of a bandage and you can actually damage a tendon and end up with a lame horse. As a safety measure, NEVER apply a bandage to a horse's leg without some cushioning, either a cotton wrap or a 'pillow-wrap', which is available at most feed stores or tack stores. Have a professional show you how to wrap a leg and practice on a fence post for the right feel. It can be very difficult to put a wrap on an injured horse that doesn't want to stand still; so the more you practice, the faster you'll get the job done when it counts.

If some proud flesh is already present from an older wound, it can be scrubbed off with gauze or even a rough sponge and some Betadine soap (surgical scrub) to prevent infection. Proud flesh must be removed in order to allow the healing of a wound but, since it doesn't have any nerve supply, your horse will not feel any pain from doing so other than the pain from the actual wound underneath. It will, however, bleed rather easily; and it is important to use clean tools and a disinfecting scrub or ointment. If you suspect that you are dealing with a case of proud flesh, feel free to go online to look at pictures for comparison and some credible advice from a veterinarian-sourced site rather than a blog where people post their own trial and error experiences. Small amounts of proud flesh can be removed by scrubbing or carefully applying a special caustic agent that will literally eat away the excessive tissue. Larger ulcerated cases will need the veterinarian's attention to sedate the horse and surgically remove the tissue. You can then proceed with disinfecting and wrapping the wound with gauze and a standing wrap until healed.

Swellings of the legs can result from kicks, bruises, or sometimes even from tiny puncture wounds that have gotten infected. Swollen legs can also simply be fluid build-up in a horse that is not moving as much as usual (e.g., when adjusting from a pasture home to a stall). This condition, called "stocked up", will resolve on its own when the horse moves around or gets worked.

As a rule, when there is heat, there is an injury. Always touch a swelling with the back of your hand to determine if there is heat present and compare with a healthy leg to be sure.

Horses are not always 3-legged lame when injured. They are pretty tough in the taking and, except for the occasional equine drama queens, they may not always display their pain obviously. As prey animals they are often hesitant to display discomfort. Being lame or sick is a sign of weakness and makes them the ones who get eaten by the wolves; so don't think your horse is not in pain just because he pretends to be happy and cheery and trying not to limp too much when moving around. It is important to know your horses and their usual behavior so that you can tell right away when something is wrong - even though they might want you to believe they're just fine!

Prolonged lameness should always be assessed by a veterinarian. There are just too many factors that can cause a horse to be lame -- some can be treated, some have to be given lots of time to heal -- and it is impossible to describe all lameness varieties in this book.

Hoof injuries

Horses' hooves are not as rock hard as they seem. Sure, the outside looks hard as a rock, but the sole is basically a soft cushion with a tough shell. Injuries to the hooves can result from wire cuts or stepping on foreign or sharp objects such as nails, which can actually cause a life-threatening injury.

If you find a nail stuck in your horse's hoof, you should call a veterinarian and NOT remove the nail unless it is absolutely necessary. If you do remove the nail, make sure to remember its location and the angle of the penetration into the hoof (or take a picture with your phone). Once you pull the nail out you might not be able to see where it was. Keep the nail to show to the vet and disinfect the area immediately. Put your horse's foot in a bucket with clean water mixed with disinfecting iodine solution.

The reason why this is so important is that the bone structure of a horse's hoof is pretty close to the sole. There is only around 1" or less of sole covering the bone inside. If an infection reaches the bone, you may have an untreatable situation on hand. A veterinarian can determine if there might be a severe problem or not by the angle and point of entry of a nail or a foreign object.

Horses that are very suddenly and severely lame on one leg, not wanting to put weight on it, may have an abscess within the hoof, which is very painful. Your farrier or veterinarian can determine if there in fact is an abscess present or if the lameness has its origins elsewhere.

If your horse stretches both front feet out in front of him and is reluctant to move or walk, there is a significant chance that he is "foundering". Founder is the advanced or untreated stage of laminitis, which is an inflammation of the laminae within the hoof. Laminitis can be brought on by a multitude of things, such as external causes (e.g., concussion on hard surface) or internal causes (ingestion of or exposure to chemicals such as fertilizer or toxic substances, overeating on fresh grass or grain, etc.) and can usually be successfully treated without lasting damage. Founder is the advanced stage of laminitis which means that the hoof structure is failing and no longer able to support the horse's weight which is extremely painful and only treatable at an early stage. Call your vet immediately if you see your horse in this awkward stance; it is an incredible amount of pain!

Choking

Horses can choke on the most inconspicuous things like a stiff weed, a carrot, or just plain hay. Ponies are prone to choking, especially miniatures. The smaller the pony, the bigger the probability of choking.

Older horses will arrive at the point where their teeth are so worn down that they can't chew their food efficiently anymore. You might hear your horse's jaw "squeak" when he eats, which means his teeth have become smooth and can no longer grind the food. In that case you will have to start soaking hay pellets instead of feeding the fresh hay in order to prevent choking.

If your horse chokes you will notice coughing or heaving, and whatever is in its mouth will come out of the nose (in case of hay, it's usually green slime). Call your veterinarian immediately and follow the instructions; try to describe what your horse ate and how long he has been in distress. A lot of times the situation will resolve on its own, but once a horse has had a choking problem it is likely to experience this problem repeatedly due to prolonged irritation and scarring of the esophagus.

Sickness / Illness

The best thing you can do is to know your healthy horse. Know his behavior, his vital signs (heart rate, temperature, breathing) when he's healthy. Horses, much like people, will react differently when ill. Some will display obnoxious behavior like pawing, stall walking, grunting or nodding or biting at the site of pain. Others will just become very quiet and try not to move, which can be easily overlooked, except the horse owner knows that his horse is "just not right" today!

One frequent indicator of illness or pain is usually lack of appetite. If your horse refuses dinner, won't take his favorite horse cookie or dips his nose into the grain bucket but won't eat, you can usually safely assume that he is trying to tell you something's wrong.

Colic

A horse's digestive tract is incredibly sensitive to changes in food, weather, regularity of feeding intervals, and other conditions. Horses do not have the ability to vomit or burp, therefore whatever is in their stomachs must go all the way through their intestines. Digestive problems are the most common reason for a horse not to feel well. They can range from a simple tummy ache to severe impaction colic in the large, or worse, the small intestine.

When your horse first displays signs of pain, you will very rarely have a way to know what caused it or how bad it will get; you need to be proactive and make sure to monitor your horse closely and find out which veterinarian is available close-by and on call after business hours.

Symptoms of colic in a horse are not always the same, but if your horse displays two or more of the symptoms listed below, you should call a veterinarian.

Symptoms:

- no appetite
- pawing or stomping at the ground with front or hind legs
- head nodding or biting the air towards the stomach area
- laying down and getting back up frequently
- restless; attempting to roll
- abnormally quiet or absent gut sounds
- elevated temperature

Colic pain usually comes in waves of mild to severe cramps, so your horse will feel miserable, 10 minutes later he may look fine and want to eat. If you suspect your horse might be colicking, DO NOT LET YOUR HORSE EAT HAY OR GRAIN. Immediately remove all the food from his paddock or stall, so he won't pack more food on top of a blockage in his gut when he feels better in between sets of cramps.

Before calling a veterinarian, you should take your horse's temperature and count his pulse and breaths per minute; this will aid your veterinarian in giving you advice over the phone before coming out. If you know what his vitals are when healthy, you can now supply the veterinarian with this information, which will help in getting a more accurate assessment of the situation in order for the veterinarian to distinguish just how distressed your horse is.

Your veterinarian will be able to tell you what to do for first measures. If you cannot reach a veterinarian right away and have to wait for a call back, here are a few things you can do in the meantime:

If your horse is willing to be led around, you can take your horse for a walk or even jog with him for a little stretch. Sometimes the movement can release trapped gas (in its most common form) and your horse will all of a sudden snap out of his pain and be back to normal. If that doesn't happen within 10-15 minutes, don't keep your aching horse trotting around. Just let him rest quietly.

If your horse is continually trying to lie down or even roll, you definitely have to keep walking him around. Lying down quietly might still be alright, but rolling or thrashing on the ground can cause a twisting of the gut and will definitely result in emergency surgery or a painful death on site.

If your horse is somewhat interested in food, you can offer a very soupy mix of what can often be a remedy for mild colic.

- 2 cups of wheat bran (tastes sweet and stimulates the intestines)
- 1 tea spoon of salt (to make them drink and stay hydrated)
- 2 cups of mineral oil (available at the feed store) - to hopefully lubricate the blockage and help to break it down.

Make sure to have *Banamine* paste on hand, an oral pain killer and muscle relaxer which is available from your veterinarian, but wait to administer until you have reached your veterinarian on the phone. Depending upon the symptoms the veterinarian may want to see your horse without the masking effects of any pain medication. If you feel you cannot reach a veterinarian and the symptoms worsen, it will definitely help your horse feel better and sometimes help resolve a very mild colic.

Gently massage the tips of your horse's ears, which are acupressure points relating to the intestines and can sometimes help.

<u>SUMMARY</u>

Obviously there are many more topics to cover, but other people have already written books about that. It's a helpful idea to have a good almanac or a horse first aid book handy that lets you look up symptoms and which explains every illness your horse could possibly have if you cannot reach help.

As a new horse owner, it would be a good idea to establish a relationship with a recommended veterinarian in your area. Being a regular client for vaccines, etc., can mean for them to work with you financially in order to enable you to get your horse treated when you need it most and that they may be happy to give you advice and answer any questions you have; be prepared that advice over the phone is not always possible without seeing your horse. If your veterinarian is not willing to spend the time to answer your questions and help educate you, you should switch your veterinarian!

Another way to keep yourself educated and to save money at the same time is to arrange for vet clinics in your area. Many veterinarians will be happy to waive their call fee or give discounts if they come to see several horses for their routine vaccinations, teeth floating, etc., at the same location and may be available for lectures on certain subjects to answer everyone's questions.

Remember that the best way to save money on vet bills is to educate yourself, be proactive in your horse care, have the necessary medical first aid kit on hand, and know a critical condition from a minor scratch.

Chapter 4

What Equipment do I need?

INTRODUCTION

Well, just having a horse standing around in the backyard is only half the fun. As a rule, don't let anyone tell you that you can't just have a horse as a companion and a pet. Horses don't come running asking us to ride them, but it is a lot of fun if your intention of having a horse at home is to also ride that horse. Typically horses are ridden on trail or in an arena of some sort (referring to a somewhat level area with or without a fence), which allows us to either exercise a horse with certain patterns and speeds or to take advantage of a fenced-in area for the rider's safety in order to practice our skills and become better riders or horsemen. Our intentions as to discipline, type of riding and expertise will then determine which tack we should buy, how much money to spend, where to save, and what is the right choice. I will describe the most common tack and what to look for; but some items are highly personalized to the horse and therefore you should ask a professional for advice.

For ease of decision making and budgeting, I have categorized each piece of equipment with letters for importance. For the purpose of this chapter, it is assumed that you intend to ride your horse!

A= Must have **B**= Good idea **C**= Optional

Halter and lead rope (A)

Halters are essential equipment when owning a horse and are used to lead your horse around in a controlled manner. They come in a few different makes and models. Most commonly you will find nylon halters, which are the most economic choice and come in an infinite variety of colors and designs.

Rope halters are a type of a halter that should only be used by experienced horsemen. A horse should never be tied to a solid object with a rope halter as they can injure the delicate nerves behind their ears if they panic.

Leather halters are a bit more expensive and will add that extra curb appeal to your horse.

Lead ropes are a personal preference – I prefer cotton lead ropes because they give the handler a better grip if the horse is unruly. A nylon lead rope comes in nicer colors but is also more slippery and can easily cause rope burns on your hands or parts of the horse if they get tangled and/or spooked.

When fitting a halter for a horse it should have a comfortable fit around his head, not too tight nor too loose. Ideally you can fit three fingers under each of the straps.

Remember that a halter should be removed when the horse is roaming freely and unsupervised (corral, stall or turnout) as they can easily catch it on a fence, tree limb, or a hook and become trapped and panicked.

If there is a reason that you must keep a halter on your horse, make sure to use a leather halter or purchase a so-called break-away halter. These halters are designed to break apart at a designated part when a great force is applied, such as a struggling horse.

Sizes: Halters are usually available in the following sizes: Foal (will fit miniature horses and small ponies), Cob (for larger ponies or small horses), Horse (for sturdy or larger type horses), Oversize (for very large breeds such as draft horses or crosses)

Where to buy: Online, feed stores, tack stores

Bridle (A)

Bridles consist of several parts that I am not going to describe in detail here. If you have no idea what a bridle is, I highly recommend that you take a few lessons from an instructor or to volunteer at a stable for a while to acquire some basic knowledge.

Bridles are typically categorized in western or english bridles, which mostly defines a certain look and style. Your horse most likely will not know the difference between the different styles, but it will definitely pay attention to the bit that is attached to the bridle you are using.

Bridles are sized similarly to halters. Depending on your horse's size you will find yourself looking for a Cob/Arab, Horse, or Oversize bridle.

Correct sizing will allow your horse to be comfortable while ridden and prevent head shaking, trying to rub, or tilting the head due to pinching or discomfort.

The browband should be large/long enough to allow your horse's ears to move freely and not be pulled forward.

The reins are a very personal choice; they should be comfortable in your hands and long enough to accommodate the length of your horse's neck. English-style reins are usually made of leather or cotton webbing; some include rubber grips or leather stops for better grip. Western reins can be made of leather, nylon, or even rope and are typically heavier than English reins. It is not essential which type of rein you choose and they are usually purchased as part of the bridle.

Bit (B)

Although there are bitless bridles available, whether your horse will respond easily to bitless riding is largely dependent upon the horse's training.

The bit will be a very important purchase as it sits in the horse's mouth and we, the riders, are using the reins to transmit signals to the horse by pulling on the reins in some fashion. Ideally your horse responds to other rider aids such as seat, legs, etc., but that will require some skill and is best learned in riding lessons.

Let's say you know how to ride and you would like to purchase a "regular" bit for your horse.

No matter if your riding style is english or western, a regular 'snaffle bit' will probably do the trick. It is gentle enough to the horse's mouth to excuse some rider error in case you pull too hard or unexpectedly on the reins, yet it is still enough to transmit your signals to the horse.

The styles, makes, models, and materials of bits on the market are endless and I will therefore not discuss all varieties here. If you would like more information; please consult a professional for advice.

Sizes: Bit size is expressed in inches, which represents the width of your horse's mouth. Ideally the bit should allow for some space on both sides of the mouth to prevent pinching and mouth sores.

Bits are sometimes very personalized choices for certain horses and you may acquire a horse that "comes with a bridle". A lot of times a horse is accustomed to or particularly agreeable to a certain bit and you can follow the advice of the previous owner if you have no reservations in doing so.

Make sure to pay attention to your horse's mouth to detect pressure points, pinched skin or more severe injuries to the inside of the mouth or tongue from an ill-fitting or unsuitable bit.

Saddle pads (A)

Saddle pads are essential equipment when using a saddle on a horse. They can prevent friction and sores and they will prolong the life of your saddle by absorbing your horse's sweat.

English saddle pads are typically made of cotton and come in different colors and designs. Additional padding can be provided by using an additional sheepskin pad or other cushioning between the cotton pad and the saddle. Western pads are usually thicker and often made of wool, foam, felt or a combination thereof to provide more padding under the saddle.

Certain saddle pads are designed to be fitted with inserts to accommodate a better saddle fit. If you are unsure what to buy, it would be good to seek the advice of a professional.

Sizes: Saddle pads are not so much divided into size as they are in style, such as contoured, padded, show quality, western, jumping or dressage.

Saddles (B)

Depending on your expectations and skill level a saddle is not necessary to ride a horse. You can ride a horse bareback (requires skill) or with a so-called bareback pad, which at the least provides cushioning (and some designs provide saddle-like support for the rider). Saddle fit will be the most important factor to keep your horse happy, healthy and structurally sound.

Consider that wearing a saddle is for a horse like wearing shoes for a person: too big and it rubs in the wrong places; too narrow and it will pinch and make it painful for the horse to move. You get the picture. After all, the horse will be asked to carry your weight for a prolonged time on its back, which can result not only in very painful soreness if the saddle does not fit correctly, but also potentially cause muscle spasms, damage to shoulder cartilage and ligaments, and lameness.

Just because your horse came with a saddle doesn't necessarily mean that it really fits if the previous owner was not savvy to fitting a saddle.

This is where you really should consult a professional to help with saddle fit if you are unsure; your horse will thank you for caring. An equine chiropractor is also usually schooled in assessing saddle fit as is a veterinarian or, even better, a professional saddle fitter (there are independent saddle fitters that do not primarily try to sell you one of their custom saddles).

However, I will try to point out the most important areas to prevent the biggest pitfalls when selecting a saddle for your horse. Saddles are mainly divided in western and english saddles, each of them offering a large variety of sub-categories.

<u>English Saddles:</u>

Jumping, all purpose, or dressage style

Unless you want to pursue a certain discipline, an all-purpose english saddle will be your best choice. If you are not familiar with the feel of an english saddle, make sure to visit a large tack store with plenty of used saddles for sale to experience the different sizes, makes and models.

Seat sizes: average size 17.5",

Tree sizes: Narrow, medium, wide and in-between sizes

<u>Western Saddles:</u>

Trail, barrel, roping, pleasure, and endurance saddles are probably the most noteworthy categories.

All these saddles have certain features that may or may not be comfortable to you personally, so I would recommend a visit to a large tack store to ask a store attendant to assist you with sitting in as many different saddles as you can to find your ideal seat size and style preference. Then you will progress to find that style saddle in your horse's size within your budget.

Seat sizes: average size 15.5" – 16"

Tree sizes: semi-quarter horse, full quarter horse bars

Remember that the tree inside any saddle has a very unique shape that will or will not correspond with the shape and length of your horse's back. Pads can be used to help adjust saddle fit if it is not perfect. Make sure to research diligently as this will determine your horse's well-being and cooperation when ridden!

Boots (B)

Any type of horse boot has the purpose of protecting different parts of a horse's legs and/or joints while ridden. Some boots are made to help them prevent stepping on themselves when doing tight or fast maneuvers; some boots are made to protect against impact from the outside, like on difficult and rocky trail rides.

Typically, prevention is always better than treating an injury, so investing in some simple "galloping boots" to protect your horse's front legs and tendons are a good idea and will help to prevent the most common injuries.

A trainer will be able to point you in the right direction for this purpose.

Polo wraps (C)

Polo wraps are used to provide flexible padding for a horse's legs, and they need to be applied with some experience as it is possible to damage a tendon with too tight of a wrap or have your horse trip over a bandage that comes loose from a leg.

Even for show horses Polo wraps are optional and are nowadays primarily used for looks as they come in many colors and designs. My advice is to be proficient in wrapping a horse's leg before using them for a prolonged period of time.

THE RIDER

As a rider, there is of course an entire fashion industry offering all kinds of clothing and specialty items to choose from. What do you really need, and what is just a bonus? I will try to help with pointing out the basics for each discipline, assuming that your goal is just to happily ride your horse on trail or in an arena. If you decide to take up showing your horse in competitions your trainer will advise you on additional gear you will need for competing.

Helmet (A)

Even though you can certainly choose to not wear a helmet, it is always advisable to never get on a horse without one. Yes, as kids we all rode without helmets and we're still alive. Yes, you think you know how to ride and won't ever fall off a horse. Yes, your horse is a senior and only walks at the speed of snail.

Helmets are not made to protect you when everything goes right. They are there to prevent you from being a vegetable if everything goes wrong.

Slipping off a horse is not usually what gets you killed. Slipping off, stepping on a rock, stumbling and falling backwards onto a tree trunk is. It's the unexpected, such as your horse tripping and falling down, your horse being stung by a wasp and starting to buck and relentlessly throwing you onto a fence or a rock – you get the picture.

After a series of professional riders suffered brain trauma from falling off their horses during freak accidents at a walk – in almost all cases the horse stumbled and didn't recover – the laws at horse shows and stables have already changed dramatically.

Western riders are still widely unsupportive of helmets because the industry has not produced a fashionable look that appeals to western riders. However, don't let a fashion statement get in the way of your or your family's safety. If you must be picky, at least use caution when getting on horses you don't know, riding in unfamiliar territory or riding by yourself. Make sure you purchase a well-fitting helmet for yourself; it will be much more comfortable and better looking than wearing your friend's!

Boots (A)

Riding boots are absolutely essential, regardless of your discipline. Although english paddock boots (or riding boots) will look very different from western riding boots, they share certain features that will help you with balance, traction, and safety.

Riding boots provide stability to your ankles, and, most importantly, have an average 1" heel that prevents your foot from slipping through the stirrup, which can result in a pretty bad injury.

If you are on a budget and need to make do with what you have, make sure that your footwear has a heel and won't in any way get stuck in the stirrup.

Never approach or lead a horse while barefoot, or in flip flops or sandals. Horses are very heavy animals and while it hurts when they step on your foot while wearing boots, it can break or crush your toe(s) if you're not wearing proper shoes.

Let a store clerk or trainer advise you on what to buy if you are unsure. Hand-me-downs from a friend or online sale items will certainly help you to save money while still acquiring necessary equipment.

Riding pants (B)

Riding pants are definitely a good idea, but you can certainly get away without owning a pair. Western riders typically wear jeans, but english riders who have a different position in a saddle will find that the seams can cause chafing; and depending on your clothing and saddle material, jeans can cause undesirable wear to your saddle as well.

However, selecting a more suitable style of jeans (stretch, flat seams and no rivets on pockets) can eliminate those worries.

If you are planning on taking lessons at a stable, riding pants are usually part of the requested attire for students; but those rules will vary.

English (Half-) Chaps (B)

Half chaps are supposed to add grip to your leg when riding and also prevent chafing from stirrup leathers in the same fashion as a tall riding boot would. The advantage is that they are removable and leave the more comfortable paddock boots (or other boots) for your daily footwear. However, many children and adults have no problem riding without half chaps, although they can definitely help in stabilizing your leg on the horse. They are designed to be worn over english riding pants or breeches, but can also be fitted over some jeans.

Western Chaps (C)

Western riders usually ride in jeans and occasionally will use leather chaps either for protection when roping or working cattle or when riding in rough terrain to protect their legs from brush. They can definitely be a fashion statement, as some of them can be customized and beautifully stamped or carved and can also add an extra layer on cold days.

Gloves (C)

Gloves will become more important the more specialized your work with the horse is. They are a good idea for english or western riders for different purposes, whether to add grip when holding your reins, prevent rope burns when working with an unruly horse, or learning how to rope. Obviously they can also just simply keep your hands warm!

Chapter 5

Which Horse is right for me?

Finally, you are all prepared, your property is perfect, and you're ready for your first horse! Of course it's usually not like that, but let's just say you live in the perfect world and you are now ready to find yourself the perfect horse.

Since this guide is designed to help mostly inexperienced horse owners, I will not describe how to find your next 5' jumper or your Grand Prix dressage horse. This is supposed to help you find a nice, loving, quiet family horse that takes you on the trail, happily lives in your backyard, and is safe to be around – believe me, it's not as easy as you might think.

First of all you have to know what it is that you would like to be doing with your horse. Are you going to share the horse with your family? Does it have to be gentle around kids? Horses are often trained for specific things. A fancy show horse might not be happy with being ridden on trail once or twice a week, and a trail horse might go lame after two months of jumping over obstacles and racing around barrels because he is not built for this kind of exercise. Some horses need a skilled rider and will not tolerate beginners on their backs. Just because the seller shows off a horse that is very quiet and well behaved doesn't mean it will stay the same with inexperienced riders and handlers such as children.

Horses come in all sizes, body shapes, breeds, abilities, and temperaments – where to start?

It can be difficult to dig through hundreds of advertisements, look at different horses, not knowing if the seller really tells the truth. Is this horse really that quiet or is he drugged? Is this horse lame or is he just a little stiff because he is older and has arthritis? Is there a difference between buying a mare or a gelding? Just because an advertised horse sounds like the perfect match does not mean it is. Typically, horses that have a lot of professional training will also have a lot of "buttons", meaning that they are used to reacting with very little input from the rider. If you are less experienced, you will be pushing these "buttons" by accident, either because your leg moves around too much or you are not that balanced on a horse. Reining horses are a good example of that. Sometimes these horses cannot adjust to a less experienced rider and become frustrated with all the wrong signals, which can lead to a grumpy attitude, bucking or biting.

If you have the budget, you should find yourself a professional trainer or a knowledgeable horse person to help you select and evaluate horses and to "test ride" them for you. A trainer will probably charge you a finder's fee, which you can negotiate in advance, but it might save you hundreds or thousands of dollars in trying to sell a horse that is not a match or overspending on a horse that is not worth its sale price, not to mention the agony of having a horse that you are not compatible with.

Horse rescues can be a wonderful resource for acquiring a horse. They are very protective of the horses that they rehabilitated with a tremendous amount of love and care and will make sure that the horse you choose is a good match for you. Often they will insist that the horse cannot be sold and has to be returned if you cannot keep it in order to ensure the further welfare of an animal that may already have been through difficult times.

Don't save money by buying a horse without obtaining a pre-purchase exam performed by a licensed veterinarian. You can save money by just having the general health and soundness of the horse looked at rather than having x-rays or other expensive exams performed. However, not only will a pre-purchase exam prevent you from buying a horse that requires expensive vet care later, it will also legally protect you should the horse have been given pain medication at the time of the vet check. It is standard policy for a veterinarian to draw blood at a pre-purchase exam in case the question of pain medication being present arises later. The blood will only be kept on file for a few weeks, and it will only be checked if you contact the veterinarian with a suspicion and ask him to do so. If the veterinarian doesn't draw blood on his own accord, be sure to insist that a blood sample is taken at the time of the exam. It can save you from ending up with a lame horse that can't be returned because you don't have proof of pain killers or tranquilizers being administered. Moreover, the veterinarian should act as your advisor. Mention in advance that you would like advice to make sure the horse is a good value for the money you are about to pay.

If you are not able to hire a trainer, make sure to be very honest about your own ability, with what you would like to use the horse for, and how it would live. Most sellers will know their horse well enough to tell you if it could be a match during the first phone call, and hopefully they are honest enough to disclose if they don't think this is so.

There is always the danger of falling in love with a horse at first sight for the wrong reasons. "His color is so gorgeous!" – "I just love his spots!" – "He was nickering when I got there!"

More importantly, a horse needs to be the right choice both for your riding skill and the discipline you have chosen. From those matches, you can narrow the decision down further by color, gender (mare or gelding), size, and breed – but don't let the perfect horse slip away because he has the wrong color hair coat!

Following are some tips for making a good choice when looking for a horse:

How to look for a family horse

Typically, a family horse that can be shared by everyone has to be very tolerant, quiet, not spooky, and safe to be around. If you are an advanced rider and the rest of your family is not, but want to be part of the horse experience, you will either have to put up with a less exciting ride on your horse or you get two different horses: One for yourself that can be more spirited, younger or more advanced in training, and one that may be older and more experienced and that will take care of your family.

Generally, any breed of horse can be a good trail horse, but it depends how comfortable you are on horseback when it comes to choosing the right temperament. Gaited horses can be a great choice because they are very comfortable to ride and usually have great endurance, but a lot of them can be quite spirited.

A family horse should be calm, gentle and respectful with people and children, not spooky, get along well with other horses, and should be older than 8 years. There are exceptions, but young horses tend to spook at things easily because they have never seen them, and can be full of energy. If you are not an experienced horse person, you should choose a middle-aged horse between 10 and 15 years old. The breed can be your personal preference, but every breed has characteristics you should consider, even though generalizing would be wrong. You can very easily determine the traits of a certain breed by spending a minimal amount of time researching this topic on the internet.

Don't take on a horse that is an active show horse needing to be retired as they might not do well with less exercise, and they are also used to a lot of activity, such as busy barns, and often don't do well in a backyard situation with little entertainment.

Key words to look for in advertisements

- Anyone can ride
- Been there, done that
- "Husband horse"
- Mounted police/patrol background (they rarely spook at anything)
- Good around kids
- Loves the trail Friendly and gentle Goes anywhere

Key words to avoid

- Light on the aids (very sensitive)
- Turns on a dime (very quick and "catty")
- Great at barrels and gymkhana (has a racing "button")
- Needs intermediate/experienced rider (really needs an experienced rider or professional)
- Still a bit green (not trained)
- Brood mare prospect (not suitable for riding or lame)
- Doesn't like _____ (lacks training, spooky, opinionated)

Obviously there are many ways to describe a horse for sale, but these are a few of the most common phrases that can give you a clue about the demeanor of the horse in question.

The Free Horse:

In tougher economic times, there are many horses that are listed as "free to a good home" because their owners are in financial distress and can no longer afford to care for their horse(s). Rescue organizations will offer horses for adoption and are often a good resource for family horses as they are honest in their descriptions and usually request that the horse be brought back if you cannot keep it any longer.

Sometimes horse owners are desperately looking for a new home for their horses, promising you everything you want to hear just to get you to take the horse.

A lot of times horse sellers/owners will agree to a "trial period" where you can pay for the horse, take it to your property, and be allowed 14 days or longer to return the horse if it doesn't work out.

It never hurts to ask for a trial period and, although it carries quite a risk for the horse owner (since the horse can get hurt in your care), most owners will agree if that's the only way the horse will get a new home. In any case you should have a good contract in place making sure all the eventualities are covered. Typically the buyer (you) will be asked to carry the risk if the horse gets injured, basically meaning "you break it - you buy it". It is a good idea to buy a short-term equine medical insurance for the horse in question which is very affordable and will cover you in case the horse gets insured or – worst case scenario – dies of an accident or sudden illness. The horse owner will likely want to inspect your property and see how and where the horse will live; or they may choose not to take this step but to be happy with having your address and maybe some photos of your place.

As you may gather from this chapter, buying and selling horses is a very personal transaction; horse owners usually have the best intentions when selling their horse and want to make sure that it will be well cared for and properly kept.

It is often very difficult for an inexperienced buyer to get a clear picture of the horse that is presented within a short appointment and a single test ride; make sure you discuss the "what if" scenario in advance.

Imagine that you buy a car and, after taking it home, it turns out that the car doesn't like the way you drive and really hates your garage!

In working with horses, riding them, or just simply being around them, you will soon find that the information pool is bottomless and that many people have many different opinions and approaches.

Not everything works for every rider or for every horse as horses are individuals with their own personalities and their own ideas.

However, because of this, your own education will be the key to success. Don't rely on your neighbor; do your own reading and research. Ask lots of questions, and one of the most important questions will be: "Why?" If you learn a certain approach, technique, or move, your teacher should always be able to tell you why it is important and why it's done the way it is done. What's appropriate for one breed or one discipline may not be applicable to another and so forth.

When looking for advice, make sure to address the best source for the subject. Let a professional trainer or veterinarian be your guide rather than that neighbor who grew up on a farm where his uncle plowed the fields with a horse. Let common sense be your guide, and consider a second and third opinion essential for getting the right answer.

Horses will enrich your life and if you approach them with an open mind, you will not only learn a lot about them but also about yourself!

I hope this book has given you a few insights in horse ownership!

Happy trails!

This book was written to encourage, to enrich, and to support the lives of horses and their owners.

Marion Wright is available online at *www.HorseSense101.com* to answer questions and offer her expertise for your specific needs.

May your journey be a successful one for you and your horse!

CPSIA information can be obtained at www.ICGtesting.com
Printed in the USA
BVOW05s2159021214

377646BV00001B/1/P